A PUBLICATION FROM
THE JAMES FORD BELL LIBRARY AT THE
UNIVERSITY OF MINNESOTA

FRANÇOIS DESERPS

A Collection of
THE VARIOUS STYLES OF CLOTHING
*which are presently worn in
countries of Europe, Asia, Africa,
and the savage islands,
all realistically depicted
1562*

Sara Shannon
EDITOR AND TRANSLATOR

INTRODUCTION BY
Carol Urness

JAMES FORD BELL LIBRARY • MINNEAPOLIS
Distributed by the University of Minnesota Press
2001

*Copyright 2001 by the James Ford Bell Library
University of Minnesota*
ALL RIGHTS RESERVED
ISBN 0-8166-4013-0

PUBLISHED WITH THE ASSISTANCE OF
THE ASSOCIATES OF THE JAMES FORD BELL LIBRARY
AND GRANTS FROM IRVING B. AND MARJORIE KREIDBERG
AND THE JOHN PARKER FUND

Designed and typeset by Brian P. Hanson

A CATALOGING-IN-PUBLICATION RECORD FOR THIS BOOK
IS AVAILABLE FROM THE LIBRARY OF CONGRESS

JAMES FORD BELL LIBRARY
UNIVERSITY OF MINNESOTA, 472 WILSON LIBRARY
309 19TH AVENUE SOUTH
MINNEAPOLIS, MINNESOTA 55455

THE VARIOUS STYLES OF CLOTHING

CONTENTS

PREFACE	VII
NOTES ON THE TRANSLATION	IX
PRODUCTION NOTE	XI
INTRODUCTION	I
REPRODUCTION AND TRANSLATION	21
NOTES	157
TRANSCRIPTIONS	161

PREFACE

Among the very rare books in the James Ford Bell Library is a copy of François Deserps's *Recueil de la diversité des habits qui sont de present en usaige tant es pays d'Europe, Asie, Affrique et Illes sauvages, le tout fait apres le naturel*, in its first edition, published by Richard Breton in 1562. In English this title is: *A Collection of the various styles of clothing which are presently worn in countries of Europe, Asia, Africa and the savage islands, all realistically depicted*. The *Recueil* is an extremely important book in that it is considered the first work published in France on costume and the first book published on ethnography. The *Recueil* consists of 121 woodcut illustrations on sixty-one leaves. Each page has a decorative border framing a figure and four lines of descriptive verse printed in *caractères de civilité*. The italic *civilité* typeface, which imitated the French handwriting of the day, was first cut and used by Robert Granjon in Lyons in 1557. Breton used the *civilité* type primarily for the publication of children's lesson-books, *belles-lettres*, music books, and books for Protestant instruction. Later and more commonly found extant editions of the *Recueil* were published in roman typeface.[1]

---

1. The mode of *civilité* type cut by Breton is larger and easier to read than Granjon's *civilité* type. Harry Carter and H. D. L. Vervliet maintain in *Civilité Types* that Breton may

In the introduction of the *Recueil*, Deserps dedicates his work to Henry of Navarre (the future King Henry IV). According to Deserps, the book was designed to teach the young prince about different peoples, places, and customs. Most of the book's illustrations depict men and women from different regions of France and Europe, along with the more exotic images of people from Asia, Africa, and South America. Some of these images are among the first representations of the latter peoples in a European publication, especially New World Indians. The book is also interesting in that it represents people of socio-economic backgrounds other than the aristocracy. The images include foot soldiers, mourners, bourgeoisie, peasants, and Indians of Brazil. Besides instructing the prince about people from other countries, the book also contains mythical figures such as a Cyclops. Other figures are exaggerated for satirical effect. Perhaps the most notable figures are those that depict bishops, priests, and monks as sea creatures. These anti-clerical caricatures and accompanying verses were no doubt meant to divert and influence the young Protestant prince. (Paris was not yet worth a mass.)[2]

have fashioned his type after another model of *civilité* type. London: Oxford University Press, 1966, p.25.

2. Henry, who had been aligned with the Protestant Huguenots, formally converted to Roman Catholicism on 25 July 1593, primarily to retain his crown. Many sources attribute to Henry the quotation "Paris is well worth a mass," but none gives a specific source for it. For information on the political and religious circumstances, see Michael Wolfe, *The Conversion of Henri IV: Politics, Power, and Religious Belief in Early Modern France.* Cambridge, MA: Harvard University Press, 1993.

NOTES ON THE TRANSLATION

My goal in translating the *Recueil* was to give a literal and accurate interpretation of the sixteenth-century French so that the reader could contemplate and enjoy the book, just as the young Henry of Navarre would have done. Unfortunately, there is no way to give the English translation the same poetic rhythm as the French version. In order to make the translation more fluid and readable in modern English, I have taken some minor liberties. The introduction of the *Recueil* was written in rambling, paragraph-long sentences, so I have broken them down into more manageable bits. Translating the poems proved to be even more challenging than translating the introduction. Every poem has four lines of verse, and each line has exactly ten syllables. In adhering to this ten-syllable structure, Deserps often omitted words or changed the verb tenses to fit the number of syllables that he needed. In some cases I have added words such as pronouns and direct objects. I have also changed some of the verb tenses. In a few cases I have put words in brackets when the meaning of a word or an omitted word was not entirely apparent.

Another poetic device used by Deserps was to make the last word in the first and third lines rhyme and the last word in the second and fourth lines rhyme. In doing so, Deserps often changed the syntax or else reversed the order of the lines, making many of the sentences grammatically incorrect. In order to compensate for this, I have changed the syntax, line order, and punctuation in many of the poems. The items in the poems which need further explanation are numbered, and found in the endnote section of the book.

Special thanks are due to Professor Carol Urness, who has been the catalyst to bring this book into print. Carol should also be thanked for the many hours that she sat with me in the library's reading room, editing my translations. Although we had many moments of exasperation over the intricacies of sixteenth-century French, we also laughed a lot. In the end we came up with a more readable and polished version of the poems. This book has also come into being through the talents of the James Ford Bell Library staff. Brian Hanson has been meticulous in the layout and design of the book. Brad Oftelie had a great vision of the book from the beginning and offered many valuable suggestions, as well as moral support. Ahn Na Brodie did an excellent job in photographing the images, and Brockman Schumacher used his computer skills to help Brian make the images even brighter and clearer. Wendy Wettergren Larson was a great assistant in proofreading the poems and spotted more than one mistake, despite our tired eyes. Others who deserve thanks are the Associates of the James Ford Bell Library, who have made this publication possible through their membership and support.

Sara Shannon
TRANSLATOR AND EDITOR

PRODUCTION NOTE

Every book takes longer to write and produce than expected. The writing, editing, and preparation for printing and binding are all steps in a process that consumes time and patience. Probably some people have produced books that were completed and printed ahead of deadlines and schedules, but these writers and volumes are not known to us. Academic publishing is slow. As an old University of Chicago Press information brochure stated: we are not making pancakes. The present book is no exception. In fact, it may hold the record for the longest book gestation period in the history of the James Ford Bell Library, aside from some books that were never published at all. The book is, we trust, worth the wait.

The idea of publishing the Deserps illustrations and poetry originated about seven years ago. In October 1993, the James Ford Bell Library at the University of Minnesota was forty years old. As part of the celebrations Dr. Ford Watson Bell, grandson of James Ford Bell and member of the Associates' Board of Directors, and Nina Archabal, Director of the Minnesota Historical Society, spoke after a festive dinner. To mark that occasion the Associates published a volume titled *James Ford Bell and His Books: The Nucleus of a Library*. This book was "unveiled" and distributed to the audience following the program. It was great fun. A special exhibit of recent acquisitions was displayed that evening, including the book that is the basis for the present one: François Deserps, *Recueil de la diversité des habits qui sont de present en usaige tant es pays d'Europe, Asie, Affrique et Illes sauvages, le tout fait apres le naturel,* Paris: de l'imprimerie de Richard Breton . . ., 1562. The title translated is *A Collection of the various styles of clothing which are presently worn in countries of Europe, Asia, Africa and the savage islands, all realistically depicted.* The book was the anniversary gift of the James Ford Bell Book Trust.

After the big celebration became memory, it was natural to consider how this special book might be shared with a broader audience. Most of the book's woodcuts featured Europeans in dress from their countries and occupations. The non-Europeans in the book are of special interest in the context of the scope of the James Ford Bell Library. Creatures like the "bishop of the sea" are especially intriguing. How could these wonderful woodcuts and their accompanying verses be reproduced in a modern book?

First, to find a translator. The professor we thought would translate the poems moved from Minnesota to Harvard University. Although it is not impossible to work with an author at a distance, it is not preferable. Sara Shannon, a favorite former student with excellent language skills, was a possible translator, but she was busy with other things. First she taught English in Korea; then she studied at the Sorbonne, and studies in medieval history at Columbia followed, leading to a Master's degree. We barely welcomed her back to the Twin Cities when she married Peter Gross and so began another phase of her life. But when she and Peter traveled to Egypt for his work, Sara took along copies of the poems and began to work seriously on translating them. From that point on Sara was engaged in bringing sixteenth-century French verses into modern English, a difficult task at best. Her commentary on the principles she used in translating the poems gives an indication — but only that — of the tremendous efforts involved.

The question of how to reproduce the beautiful hand-colored woodcuts for the book was a major concern. Early attempts to reproduce the illustrations using standard photographic equipment (the 4 x 5 camera used for most black-and-white photography) were disappointing. The colors were difficult to capture; the "bleed-through" of color from one page to the next was distracting. The predicted costs were astronomical. The process of identifying specifications for a digital camera that would meet our needs was not easy, but Jon Nichols, head of Information Technology Services, used his expertise to discover the right camera. The digital camera arrived after what seemed a very long time, and we began to see the potential of using this new technology. For the Deserps woodcuts, Bruce Bruemmer, of the Digital Technology Department, designed a special mechanism to hold the book while it was being photographed. This device was dubbed the "deserperator." Bruce and Ahn Na Brodie, photographer, managed to produce the fine photographs that are the foundation for this book. At last the illustrations were photographed and on disk.

The next step was to edit the illustrations to make them as close as possible to the originals. This was not done to change the illustrations but instead to clear up backgrounds, remove stains or bleed-through from the opposite side of pages, and sharpen images as needed to make them look as they did when they were printed and painted. To this effort Brian Hanson, word processor, and Brock Schumacher, student assistant, devoted many hours. The book was mercifully short, but the editing done on the illustrations was tedious and sometimes frustrating, at very best. When it was all over the woodcut images appeared like the originals. From the beginning the intention was made to keep the appearance of the book as close to the 1562 printing as possible, with the illustrations and verses left in their original format and the English translations placed below them. The transcriptions and notes were placed at the end of the text in order to maintain the desired format. P. J. Kulisheck provided some excellent reference help in the final stages of editing the book.

All of this has taken longer than anyone expected. But it was a labor of love, not of necessity. The translator received no pay for her labors. No staff member was paid anything extra for working on the book. Deserps has been a "when time is available" project. Irving B. and Marjorie Kreidberg and the Associates have subsidized its publication, which has helped enormously. We thank everyone who was involved in the book and its production, especially Sara Shannon and Brian Hanson. They were the crucial people involved in the publication of this book.

Carol Urness, Curator
JAMES FORD BELL LIBRARY

INTRODUCTION

The saying that "clothes make the man" dates from the early fifteenth century, apparently. Living in today's society, in which people often give great attention to their appearance, whether seeking to look "casual" in designer blue jeans or chic in special "black tie" clothing, one can easily say that attitudes have not changed. Most of us have favorite outfits. Some of us "dress for success" or wear "power colors" or "our" colors for special occasions. Young adults are acutely aware of style and its importance in their clothing. They may feel that their social life depends on what they wear. Even those women and men who claim to have little interest in what they wear are apt to observe carefully the styles of clothing worn by members of audiences at concerts and theaters. Some women wonder how it could be that they wear long skirts — cheerfully — that would seem more appropriate to their grandmothers and great-grandmothers. Devotion to appearance is nothing new. In earlier centuries people who could afford fine clothes wore them. Some colors and fabrics were restricted to those of certain economic or social status. Style in clothing was important, and people were identified with their occupation by their clothing. In our own day, even with a decidedly casual approach to dress we expect policemen and women, post office workers, doctors, and ambulance drivers to be wearing clothes that reflect their occupations.

This book can teach us much about clothing, and its significance in the mid-sixteenth century. It was a time of change in clothing. European explorations had opened a new world for commerce and thus for fashion. Long-distance trade by sea made some fabrics, for example cotton, much more widely available. Venice, which had in the fifteenth century become a center for luxury fabrics by using imported silk from the Orient, had to face competition in this trade. Foreign fabrics of exotic patterns and colors appeared with greater regularity on European markets. As Daniel Defoe later put it so well: "Fashion is truly termed a witch; the dearer and scarcer any commodity, the more the mode."[1] Dressing the human body in the finest fabrics and the latest fashion was a possibility, if not a mandate. Royalty set the style; the upper classes imitated. Clothing was functional, yes, but even more, clothing was costume, a decoration of the human body. Clothing linked the wearer to a geographical area, to a social status, and often to an occupation. A brief background on the colors, fabrics, and styles of clothing shown in Deserps is useful for enjoying this book.

FABRICS

Most European clothing in the sixteenth century was made from wool, linen, cotton, or silk.

---

1. Daniel Defoe, *The Naked Truth, in an Essay upon Trade*, 1696, quoted in M. D. C. Crawford, *The Heritage of Cotton: The Fibre of Two Worlds and Many Ages*. New York: Putnam, 1924, p. 98.

Wool and flax were common materials that had been known and woven into cloth for centuries. Many cloths were made of wool, in a wide variety of fabrics depending on the methods of processing, cleaning, carding, spinning, and then weaving used in their production. The difference between simple shearing, combing, and weaving at home for family use and the more complex processing and weaving for commercial consumption resulted in cloth with differing qualities, from rough to very fine. Worsted, sateen, and damask — all are terms that have referred to wool cloth at one time or another. Even the names of wool fabrics may have variant meanings. For example, the word *kersey* refers to two kinds of woolen cloth — one a ribbed cloth often used for stockings and trousers and the other a twilled fabric, at times with cotton added, that was made into coats. The illustrations in Deserps often show the wearers in heavy clothing, patterned and finely decorated with jewels or with embroidery or lace, sometimes striped or plaid. The fabric in this clothing is usually wool, which served to clothe both the rich and the poor. Wool was very attractive, inexpensive, widely available, and warm.[2]

Linen is made of flax by a process that was known to the Egyptians as early as 4000 B.C. The stems of flax, when processed and spun, produce a fine material. One of many references to cloth-

---

2. On the Spanish wool trade see Carla Rahn Phillips and William D. Phillips, Jr., *Spain's Golden Fleece: Wool Production and the Wool Trade from the Middle Ages to the Nineteenth Century*. Baltimore: The Johns Hopkins University Press, 1997.

ing cited in Homer's *Iliad* is the following: "But rousing himself from sleep, the divine voice swirling round him, Atrides sat up, bolt awake, pulled on a soft tunic, linen never worn, and over it threw his flaring battle-cape, under his smooth feet he fastened supple sandals, across his shoulder slung his silver-studded sword."[3] The Romans introduced linen into England and the Low Countries, where the climate was ideal for growing the long-stemmed flax that made the finest and strongest cloth. Popular in France as well, centuries later flax seeds traveled with the French to New France. The English introduced the plant to New England. Today linen is enjoying a renaissance in popularity as a fabric for clothing.

Linen was more commonly used in clothing than cotton was in sixteenth-century Europe. Shirts and blouses, decorative aprons, ruffs and scarves were made of linen. All of these are shown in the illustrations of Deserps. Luxury fabrics were created from linen, for example, a linen damask (a rich, patterned cloth) was made by weaving the linen threads in different directions. A "taffeta" or glossy cloth was made from linen, according to *The Oxford English Dictionary*. Linen is versatile. It could be dyed. Designs could be printed on it using carved wood blocks to make the designs, sometimes with several blocks for different colors. Each color was printed separately with its own block.

3. Homer, *The Iliad*, translated by Robert Fagles, Introduction and notes by Bernard Knox. New York: Viking Penguin, 1990, p. 100, 2-lines 49-51.

The Various Styles of Clothing

Linen was used for the ruff, the pleated neck frill that was introduced to France in 1533 when Catherine de Médici married Henry II. It is probably no surprise that France was a leader in fashion in the sixteenth century, and this style later spread to other European cities. The history of the ruff is not well studied, but the ruff became larger later in the sixteenth century, so that in 1583 Philip Stubbes commented that when fashionable ladies are caught out in the rain "their great ruffes strike sayle and flutter like dish-clouts about their neckes."[4] Look for fancy shirts, headdresses, blouses, and sleeves in the Deserps illustrations. The cloth in all of them probably is linen. Even the sails for the ships of European explorers were made of flax.

Cotton was rarer in the sixteenth century. At the end of the fifteenth, the Europeans who knew cotton best were the Spaniards, due to their relations with the Moors, and the Italians, because of their trade to the east. From early in the fourteenth century, however, a modest trade between Venice and Ulm and other cities in southern Germany developed, involving the addition of cotton to linen and woolen cloth, for fabrics known as "fustians", "barchents", "ripplecht", and "gehorte".[5] England imported these fabrics in the fourteenth and fifteenth centuries. Designs in multiple colors were printed on them with wooden blocks, each carved to produce one color of the design.

4. *Shakespeare's England: An account of the Life and Manners of his Age*. Oxford: Clarendon Press, 1962, c. 1916. II:93.
5. Crawford, *Heritage of Cotton*, p. 82.

These fabrics were expensive and difficult to get, and therefore very desirable.

When Christopher Columbus arrived in the West Indies, he saw people there wearing cotton clothing, which helped to convince him that he had reached India. Cotton was being harvested at the time, and Columbus brought cotton back with him on his return to Spain.[6] Not long after this, the Portuguese and Dutch voyages to India and the East Indies opened a trade route for the importation of cotton fabrics. Once the routes for Indian Ocean trade in cotton were open, the demand grew and the trade increased. Much of this happened after the time of Deserps, when cotton was still a rarity in most of Europe. But some of the fabrics shown in the book may well be cotton. By late in the seventeenth century, Defoe noted that it had taken over the clothing of people of all social ranks. "Nor was this all, but it crept into our houses, our closets, and bed-chambers; curtains, cushions, chairs and at last, beds themselves, were nothing but callicoes or Indian stuffs; and in short, almost everything that used to be made of wool or silk, relating either to the dress of women or the furniture of our houses, was supplied by the Indian trade."[7]

Silks and velvets, the ultimate in luxury fabrics, came from Italy or France at the beginning of the fifteenth century. Silk originated in China about forty-five hundred years ago. For centuries the secret of silk production was safe, since the

6. *Ibid.*, p. 30.
7. *Ibid.*, p. 99.

silk moth and the white mulberry, the food of the moth, were confined to China. For at least twenty-five hundred years after its discovery, silk remained a product solely Chinese. No one else knew how to make it. In 552 A.D. two Persian monks brought the eggs of the silkworm out of China by concealing them in their canes.[8] Soon silk production in Persia reached high levels. With the conquest of Persia by Alexander the Great the secret passed to the Greeks. In the Roman empire the cost of silk was equal to that of gold and pearls. Then only queens and princesses could afford to wear pure silk.

By the sixteenth century in Europe, silk was worn by royalty and anyone else who wanted to wear it and who could afford it. As Philip Stubbes complained in 1583 "it is impossible to know who is noble, who is worshipful, who is a gentleman, who is not, because all persons dress indiscriminately in silks, velvets, satens, damaskes, taffeties and such like notwithstanding that they be both base by birth, and servile by calling, and this I count a great confusion and a general disorder, God be merciful unto us."[9] The chief source for silks and velvets was still Italy, which specialized in costly silk and mixed silk fabrics, sometimes interwoven with silver and gold. The prices were outrageously high, yet did not decrease their attraction or slow their sale. Colors were very beautiful, from the strong colors preferred by the Eng-

---

8. John Feltwell, *The Story of Silk*. New York: St. Martin's Press, 1990, pp. 8-9.
9. *Shakespeare's England*, II:103.

lish court to the more subtle hues in favor in the French and Spanish courts.[10] Royalty set the fashion; others imitated and copied the fashions of the court. According to Deserps, merchants changed their style in dress the least.

Several other materials used in clothing are shown in the Deserps illustrations, particularly in the accessories worn by the people depicted in them. Many hats are made from or decorated with feathers, furs, and leather. The helmets, armor, and shields of soldiers are made of leather or metal. For both men and women the fashions in shoes range from none at all to cloth, leather, and wooden shoes. Women sometimes had clogs as "outside" shoes and fancier "inside" shoes, made of cloth and leather, often with slightly pointed toes. A few illustrations show gloves, which were extremely expensive at the time. Some women have purses or pomanders (containers for mixtures of aromatics and disinfectants like musk and ambergris to protect against odor and infection) hanging from their belts. Men wore them as well at the time, but no illustration in Deserps depicts a man with a pomander. The women carry a variety of baskets, sometimes with eggs or other food. Some of the women have children with them. Animals are included: a chicken rides on a woman's shoulder; an African girl and the woman of Pamplona hold dogs; a woman carries a basket of eggs and two ducks; a falconer has his bird on his glove. The woman of Lyons plays a lute, another woman has a tambourine. Two of the figures carry books.

10. *Ibid.*, II:101.

These are touches that make these people come alive to the modern viewer, after more than 450 years.

❧ COLOR

The reader will soon note that many of the illustrations reproduced from Deserps are only partially colored. This is how they appear in the original book, often with just touches of color or parts of the figures in color. The colors are blue, primarily, with several shades of brown, orange and reddish-orange, grey, and bits of green. Blue dominates, and even the foliage painted in the illustrations usually has a bluish cast.

Readers familiar with hand-colored illustrations and maps from the sixteenth century will recognize the blues, reds, and greens that were employed in coloring the Deserps. From the early period until the nineteenth century, when synthetic dyes were developed, the pigments used in watercolors came from the same sources as dyes for cloth. The choice of colors had increased with time. Stone Age artists had only red earth, yellow earth, carbon black, and chalk white for their paintings. A green from malachite, blue from azurite, a cinnabar red, and the deep and lovely indigo blue were available to Egyptian artists.[11] The madder plant served the Egyptians as the source of Alizarin red used for fabrics and in watercolor paintings. Insects and mollusks were also used to make pigments for watercolor painting. Some of

---

11. Jenny Rodwell, *Watercolorist's Guide to Mixing Colors*. Cincinnati: North Light Books, 1997, p. 13.

these were extremely rare — for example, it took many thousands of the small *Murex* shellfish to produce enough Tyrian purple dye for a single Roman robe. Lapis lazuli, ground and made into a paste with oil and gum, made the most highly prized ultramarine blue. The choice of colors available on the palette of a sixteenth-century watercolorist was limited. Near the end of the eighteenth century many new colors became available from minerals and by more experimentation in producing colors.

The many colors available today would astonish the sixteenth-century dye-master, who would be even more surprised by the wide availability of some colors. For example, in earlier centuries indigo blue could be worn only by the wealthy, as the plant material from which this dye was made was difficult to grow, process, and transport. Now indigo blue can be seen in jeans anywhere in the world because of the synthetic production of it developed in nineteenth-century Germany. The history of how indigo was planted in several parts of the world by Europeans is told in John Parker, *The World for a Marketplace: Episodes in the History of European Expansion* (Minneapolis: Associates of the James Ford Bell Library, 1978, pp. 183-196). The number of dyes presently known is incredible: by 1980, for example, about three *million* dyes were available.[12] Still more astonishing, the National Bureau of Standards estimates that the

---

12. Commentary from *Watercolor Color, in association with the Royal Academy of Arts*, Ray Smith, editor. London: Royal Academy of Arts, 1993, pp. 6-9.

human eye can distinguish approximately *ten* million different colors!

The colors used by the watercolorist in the Deserps illustrations presumably follow the colors of the original clothing, but that is difficult to know, for perhaps the watercolorist had no indications of color to follow. And it is difficult to know to what extent the colors used for the illustrations may have been dictated by factors of availability, cost, and time. Since the book was intended for a broad audience, particularly youngsters, cost and speed may have been a deciding factor in the number of colors used in the book. And, unfortunately, the verses seldom mention the colors of the clothing illustrated.

FASHION

European fashions changed much from the fifteenth to the mid-sixteenth century. In earlier times most countries had little contact with each other. With the rise of long-distance trade the style popular in one area might well be adopted in another, many miles away. Cities like London became centers of consumption; cities like Venice, Genoa, Florence, Lyons, and Paris gained enormous wealth through trade.[13] This wealth was displayed in clothing of heavy, sumptuous fabrics decorated with lace, pearls and other jewels, embroidery, and patterns. Attempts to curtail the use of gold and silver as decoration for clothing were

13. François Boucher, *20,000 Years of Fashion: The History of Costume and Personal Adornment.* New York: Henry Abrams, Inc., 1966, p. 221.

doomed to failure, apparently, as Spain passed sumptuary laws in 1515, 1520, 1523, and 1534. France passed similar laws in 1532 and 1554, with the same lack of success.

Fashions crossed national boundaries. For example, men from several European countries are depicted wearing close-fitting doublets — jackets with or without sleeves — stiffened with wood, metal, or whalebone.[14] Women from various countries are shown in tight-fitting bodices. Some styles called for tight sleeves, often with decorations or small puffs at the shoulders. Collars with frills were fashionable for both sexes in the mid-sixteenth century. Cloaks of various lengths are common in the Deserps images; coats, with or without sleeves, are shown.

In France beards and short hair were popular because the King had an injury and as a result shaved his head.[15] In several European countries women painted their faces. In their hairstyles women sometimes curled their hair over a pad at the forehead, and then pulled it back on their head. Often they dyed their hair. Wigs were common and women wore jewels and other decorations in their hair. Hats for both men and women were fashionable and often quite elaborate and interesting.

Men wore long stockings with their shoes or boots, which often were styled with slightly-pointed toes. The stockings of both men and women were made of fine yarn, usually worsted

14. *Shakespeare's England*, II:95.
15. *Ibid*, p. 233.

wool. Silk stockings were known but were rare and costly. The first silk stockings were not introduced in England until 1560, and then as a gift to Queen Elizabeth. In this period neither women nor men wore underwear. For women, the farthingale was a new style in the sixteenth century. Invented by the Spanish, it was introduced to the French in the first half of the sixteenth century. Others adopted it from the French example. A round petticoat made from canvas covered with taffeta or other material over a frame of whalebone, cane hoops, or metal strips, the farthingale was worn under a skirt of brocade, cloth, or velvet.[16] In the latter part of the century farthingales became much larger than the ones that are shown by Deserps.

Women and men commonly wore rings, gold for those who could afford it, and brass, silver, or pewter for others. Both men and women wore gloves, if they could afford them. In the few images where Deserps shows someone with gloves, they are generally holding them tightly in their hands! Depending on their status and occupation, the men carried a sword or a dagger.

In matters of fashion, the origin of clothing was noteworthy. For example, in *The Merchant of Venice*, Portia describes her English admirer's clothing: "I think he bought his doublet in Italy, his round hose in France, his bonnet in Germany."[17] The desire to be "in style" was remarked

16. *Ibid.*, II:94.
17. William Shakespeare, *The Merchant of Venice*, 1594, edited by W. Moelwyn Merchant. Harmondsworth, Middle-

upon by Shakespeare in the *Taming of the Shrew*, as follows:

> With silken coats and caps and golden rings,
> With ruffs and cuffs and farthingales and things;
> With scarfs and fans and double change of bravery,
> With amber bracelets, beads, and all this knavery.[18]

In his book, François Deserps illustrates clothing from Europe, Africa, Asia, and America showing that the love of style was not restricted to gender or place. As George Crabbe (1754-1832) put it so well:

> Fashion, though Folly's child, and guide of fools,
> Rules e'en the wisest, and in learning rules.[19]

☙ HISTORY

In 1562, the year the Deserps book was published, France was in the midst of religious upheaval because of discord between Catholics and Protestants. Henry of Navarre, the future King Henry IV (reigned 1589-1610) to whom the book is dedicated, was eight years old. He had been brought to court the previous year as a potential heir to the throne, as the grandson of Margaret, sister to King Francis I, who reigned 1515-1547. Henry was initially instructed in the Protestant religion but then later in the Catholic religion.

sex: Penguin, Act I, Scene I, Lines 69-71.

18. William Shakespeare, *The Taming of the Shrew*, ca. 1592-94, edited by H.J. Oliver. Oxford: Clarendon, 1982, Act IV, Scene III, Lines 55-58.

19. *The Oxford Dictionary of Quotations*, fifth edition, edited by Elizabeth Knowles. Oxford: Oxford University Press, 1999, 243:1.

Henry II, the eldest son of Francis I, died in 1559. Two more sons, Charles IX (1560-1574) and Henry III (1574-1589) would reign as king of France before Henry of Navarre became king. Throughout this period the royal family was divided in religion. Anti-Catholic sentiments are obvious in some of the verses that Deserps writes.

The sources that Deserps used for the illustrations in this book are unknown. Artists had portrayed — in scenes or in portraits — the clothing of European peoples from an early date, but it would be difficult to know how many of these Deserps might have been able to see. Drawings and woodcuts by Albrecht Dürer (1471-1528) and Hans Holbein (1460-1524) could have inspired some of the Deserps images. Published illustrations in books had a wider circulation. Deserps may well have been inspired by the woodcut illustrations showing people in early books like Hartmann Schedel (1440-1514), *Registrum huius operis libri cronicarum cum figuris et ymaginbus ab inicio mundi*, published in Nuremberg by Anton Koberger in 1493, (the "Nuremberg Chronicle"); Bernhard von Breydenbach (d. 1497), *Peregrinatio in Terram Sanctam*, published in Mainz by Erhard Reuwich in 1486; or editions of the *Travels* of Sir John Mandeville.

Books showing illustrations of people, published prior to 1562, may have inspired Deserps, but so far as is known presently they were not copied by him. The folio *Cosmographia: Beschreibung aller Lender* by Sebastian Münster, published first in a German edition (Basel: Henrich Petri,

1544; followed by other editions and translations) has many woodcuts showing people from various parts of Europe, as well as some woodcuts depicting people of other continents. The illustrations in this widely-circulated book were not copied by Deserps. Books describing travel to particular areas often had illustrations. The widely-published book by Olaus Magnus, Archbishop of Uppsala (1490-1557), describes northern peoples and places. The first French translation, printed in Paris in 1561, is titled *Histoire des pays septentrionaus*. It includes illustrations of Danes, Finns, Greenlanders, Lapps, Norwegians, and Swedes. Deserps used none of these images in his work. The most widely-known book about Africa available in the time of Deserps was written by Leo Africanus (ca. 1492 – ca. 1550). The first French edition of it is *Description de l'Afrique* (Lyons: Jean Temporal, 1556). This printing includes accounts of travel to Africa of Lodovico Varthema (fifteenth century) and Alvise Cadamosto (1432-1488). In addition to text, the book has illustrations of people from Egypt, Ethiopia, Senegal, and "l'Arabie heureuse" but these images have not been copied by Deserps, either. Another popular writer, Andre Thevet, was a member of Admiral Coligny's unsuccessful Huguenot colony in Brazil. He wrote an account of it titled *Les singularitez de la France antarctique, autrement nommee Amerique, & de plusieurs terres & isles decouuertes de nostre temps* (Paris: heritiers de Maurice de la Porte, 1557). Thevet wrote another illustrated book, *Cosmographie de Levant* (Lyons: Jan de Tournes, et Guil.

Gazeau, 1554). Presumably Deserps would have known of these books, and particularly any published in Paris. He may have seen these books but he did not copy images from any of them.

Deserps informs us in his Dedication that "I followed some sketches made by the deceased Roberval, Captain for the King, and from a certain Portuguese having frequented many and diverse countries; also from those which we see daily with our own eyes." The last is clear, though how many countries did Deserps visit, and how many people from England, Scotland, or Egypt visited Paris? Probably very few but at least some. The reference to Roberval is intriguing. Jean François de La Rocque, Sieur de Roberval, lived from 1500 to 1560, so the "deceased" is accurate for the date that Deserps wrote. Roberval was a Protestant with a Calvinist background. The religious atmosphere in France was leading to a crisis, and apparently Roberval had spent a good deal of money at the French court. He decided to recoup his losses and escape persecution by traveling to Canada. Taking part in a colonization project headed by Jacques Cartier, a Catholic, became a near obsession for him. "His imagination had been inflamed by the tales of Cartier, and the New World had become the sole object of his thoughts." In 15 January 1541 Roberval was named "lieutenant general" of the expedition to Canada.[20]

20. About Roberval's life see H. P. Biggar, *A Collection of Documents relating to Jacques Cartier and the Sieur de Roberval* Ottawa: Public Archives of Canada, 1930 and Emile Morel,

Cartier had begun preparations for his third voyage to Canada the previous year, and sailed in May 1541. Roberval, meanwhile, waited for guns and ammunition, which were not received until September of that year, so he missed the sailing season. To pass the time, it seems that Roberval may have participated in some piracy. He finally departed from France in April 1542, arriving in Newfoundland on 8 June, where he met Cartier a few days later. Roberval ordered Cartier to return westward with him up the St. Lawrence River. Cartier disobeyed the order, sailing for home during the night, and Roberval was left to continue an expedition — which was unsuccessful — into the interior of Canada alone. Roberval returned to France in the fall of 1543, with his fortune now entirely spent. In 1548 he was placed in charge of all mining operations in France, a position he held until his death in Paris, probably early in 1561. Did Deserps and Roberval meet?

A brief account of the Roberval expedition is found in Richard Hakluyt's *The principall navigations, voiages and discoveries of the English nation. . . .* (London, 1600, vol. III:240-1). No illustrations accompany the text printed by Hakluyt and there is no mention of any drawings made during the expedition. The text indicates that Cartier had discovered "Diamontes and a quantitie of Golde ore" and that they wanted to have the glory of the discoveries for themselves, which was the reason

"Jean-François de La Rocque, Seigneur de Roberval, Vice-Roi du Canada" in *Bulletin de la Société Historique de Compiègne* 8 (1895): 5-48.

The Various Styles of Clothing

that they "stole privily away the next night from us" (p. 240). Roberval was at St. John's for most of June, partly because the expedition was taking on fresh water and "partly because in composing and taking up of a quarrel betweene some of our Countreymen, and certaine Portugals" (p. 241). Could Roberval have met some Portuguese who was the source of the drawings that were passed on to Deserps? It is at best a possibility, but a very interesting one.

The "certain Portuguese" reference is challenging if it referred to published works, since the possible sources are limited. If the illustrations were not published, it would be curious that Deserps had access to them. If they were published, the likely sources would be books by men like Lodovico de Varthema (fifteenth century); Fernão Lopes de Castanheda (d. 1559); or Antonio Galvão (d. 1557). None of the books by these writers have illustrations that relate to Deserps. So, the mystery remains.

In the end the Deserps *Recueil* leaves us with several questions that cannot be answered at this time. What sources did Deserps use for the illustrations in his book? That is not known. We do not know whether he had manuscript drawings or if he used descriptions found in texts. The verses are simple, as though the reader is being taken through a photograph album of people from various parts of the world. Translated into English, in spite of all attempts to make them otherwise, the verses are repetitive and often not informative. The woodcuts are not of high quality in comparison to some — for example by Albrecht Dürer — and yet they are charming in their own way. The year 1562 is long ago. How did people learn about each other without radio or television, without the internet, without photographs or motion pictures? Today, travelers visit some of the remotest places on the planet, carrying cameras and camcorders. This book reminds us that people long ago had as great a curiosity about "others" as we do today. What do people in Turkey look like? What do they wear? How are they like us, and how are they different? Deserps gives us a rare opportunity to see, through his eyes, illustrations of people from his time and to enjoy or endure his comments in verse about them.

Carol Urness, Curator
JAMES FORD BELL LIBRARY

REPRODUCTION AND TRANSLATION

FRANÇOIS DESERPS

A collection of
the various styles

of clothing, which are presently
worn in countries of Europe,
Asia, Africa and the savage
islands, all realistically depicted.

Paris.
From the printer of Richard Breton, Rue
G. Jacques, à l'Escreuisse. 1562.
With the privilege of the King.

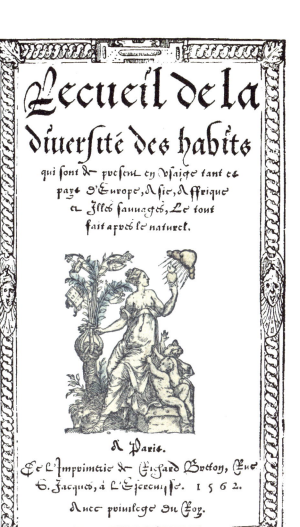

To the Reader,

Concerning the diversity of clothing which is represented in the present book.

If you wish to see some realistic portraits of women, girls and men, gestures and styles of clothing of our present time, read this book with affection and to gain a contented spirit. As you look over these portraits, you will clearly recognize that people make extraordinary garments which differ one from the other.

Au lecteur,

Sur la diuersité des habits contenus en ce present liure.

Si tu veux voir & femmes, filles,
 & hommes,
Plusieurs pourtraicts, le geste, & vestement,
Au naturel, en ce temps ou nous sommes,
Pour recevoir d'esprit contentement,
Ly en ce Liure affectueusement,
Et ton regard dessus ces pourtraicts rangé,
Tu cognoistras Les habits clairement,
Qui Les humains font L'vn & L'autre
 estrange.

To the very illustrious Prince Henry of Bourbon, son of the King of Navarre, [from] François Deserpz his very humble and obedient servant. Health and happiness [to you] forever.

You are duly informed by the lesson of the Holy Scriptures (most illustrious Prince) that our first fathers were clothed in leaves, and pelts, only to cover the nudity of their bodies. But little by little, as men became more mischievious with the age, this clothing was changed in many and diverse ways. This came about as much by necessity as by human curiosity, as is seen in Northern countries where the inhabitants are obliged to dress in fur or heavy coats, and in the Southern countries where they are nude or dressed in light clothes. The savages and Brazilians in these countries confirm this, even when the sun is near Cancer. When there is a necessity to defend themselves or to attack others, they are compelled by such circumstances to arm themselves in chain mail or to put on leather vests. This would

A tresillustre Prince,

Henry de Bourbon, fils du Roy de Navarre, François Desprez, son treshumble & tresobeissant seruiteur, Salut et felicité perpetuelle.

Vous estes deuement

aduerty par la leçon des liures saincts (Prince tresillustre) que noz premiers peres estoyent vestus de fueilles & de peaux, pour couurir la nudité de leur corps seulement : mais peu à peu, croissant auec l'aage, la malice des hommes, on a changé ces habits premiers en plusieurs & diuerses manieres, Ce qui est aduenu tant par necessité que par curiosité des humains, comme il se voit que es pays Septentrionnaux les habitans sont contraincts de se vestir d'habits fourrez ou grosses mantes, & au pays Meridionnal sont nudz, ou vestus à la legere, comme cela se peult verifier par les Sauuages & Bresiliens, mesmes en ces pays, Lors que le So-

a ij

be of little consequence in itself, but curiosity has surpassed the necessity of producing such a great difference in clothing, as much for the masculine as for the feminine sex, which in a strange way has put everyone in wonder, when considering the diverse styles worn by the people of this century.

Now in my opinion, diversity has come about on the one hand, because of different religions, and on the other hand, because of a curiosity about people and far away countries. Further, arrogance and presumption have completed this role. It can best be considered in this way, as I can not make known without a long discourse. For this reason (my lord) I have made this Collection depicting the diversity of clothing which is presently in use in Europe, Asia, Africa as well as in the islands of savages and cruelty. I have followed some sketches made by the deceased Roberval, captain for the King, and from a certain Portuguese having frequented many and diverse countries; also from those which we see daily with our own eyes. I have

teil est prochain du Cancer, et quand à la necessité de se defendre ou assaillir, cela a contrainct ceulx de tel exercice de s'armer, mailler, ou prendre collet de buffe. Ce seroit peu de chose de cela, mais la curiosité surmontant la necessité a engendré une si grande difference d'habits, tant au sexe masculin, que feminin, que telle façon estrange a mis tout homme en admiration, considerant les modes diverses dont sont vestus les hommes de ce siecle. Or quant a la diversité, selon mon iugement la difference des religions en a engendré une partie, et la curiosité des personnes, et la distance des pays, une autre partie, plus l'arrogance & presomption ont accreu ce roolle, ainsi que le pourrez mieux considerer, que ie ne le puis declarer, sans en faire vn long discours. A ceste cause (Monseigneur) i'ay fait ce Recueil contenant la diversité des habits qui sont à present en vsage, tant en Europe, Asie, Affrique, que és Isles des Sauuages et Barbares, ayant suiuy quelque dessein

dared to make you a modest gift of this Collection, with no other hope than that of serving you indefinitely. Nevertheless (my lord) I am convinced that you will not think it good that I take trouble or pleasure in making something unedifying. But I hope that you will receive some enjoyment in seeing the fickleness of our ancient predecessors, and see that they were more particular about luxurious clothing than rare virtue. One can see that many are well honored by the number and sumptuousness of their clothing and yet are empty of virtue and sound conscience. And it seems that they are of the race of hypocritical pontiffs, or from that wicked rich man mentioned in the book of Saint Luke, who was dressed in purple and silk, while poor Lazarus died from hunger at his door. This example can serve us and rid us of all extravagant dress which makes men proud: because in the same way that we all recognize the monk in frock, the fool in fool's cap, the soldier in arms, so we recognize the wise man in clothes which are not extravagant. I do not intend, how-

The Various Styles of Clothing

du defunct Sobrual, capitaine pour le Roy, & d'vn certain portugois ayant frequenté plusieurs & diuers pays, semblablement & ceux que nous voyons iournellement à l'œil, Duquel recueil i'ay bien osé vous faire humble present, non sous autre esperance sinon de vous faire perpetuel seruice, toutefois (Monseigneur) ie me suis persuadé que vous ne trouuerez pas bon que i'aye pris peine ou plaisir à faire chose non edificatiue: Mais i'espere que vous receurez quelque contentement d'y voir la mobilité de noz vieux predecesseurs, & qu'ils ont esté plus curieux & somptueuse vesture que de estre vertu, ce qui se peult cognoistre en ce que plusieurs sont fort esmeuz pour la multitude & somptuosité de leurs vestemens, & toutefois sont vuydes de vertu & saine conscience. Et semble qu'ils soyent de la race des pontifes pharisiens, ou de ce mauuais riche mentionné en sainct Luc, qui estoit vestu de pourpre & de soye, & ce pendant le pauure Lazare mouroit de faim à sa porte. Cest exemple (dy-ie) nous peult

a iij

ever, to scorn the excellent clothes of those who are worthy of wearing them, in order to enhance their prerogative and magnificence, nor the stones or precious jewels given by the Creator to amuse the hearts of his creatures. It is my hope that no one becomes attached to these things, but rather to know the true cornerstone, Jesus Christ, upon whom the true Church of God is founded, and that it be embellished with gold and fine metal, that is to say by an active faith opened by charity in Jesus Christ our only Savior. To whom I pray whole-heartedly to maintain and preserve you throughout a long and prosperous life.

seruir & retrancher toute excessiue vesture, qui attire l'homme à ouguetil: car tout ainsi qu'on cognoist le Moyne au froc, le fol au chapperon, & le soldat aux armes, ainsi se cognoist l'homme sage à l'habit non excessif, ie n'entens toutefois mespriser les habits excellens & ceux qui sont dignes de les porter, pour descoure leur prerogatiue & magnificence, ne les pierreries, & ioyaux precieux donnez du Createur, pour recreer le cueur & ses creatures: mais ie desire que nul n'y attache son affection, ains en la vraye pierre angulaire, à sçauoir Jesus Christ, sur laquelle est fondée la vraye Eglise de Dieu, & qu'elle soit enrichie d'or & fin esmail, c'est à dire de viue foy ouurante par charité en Jesus Christ nostre Sauueur vnique. Lequel ie prie affectueusement vous maintenir & conseruer en longue connualescence & prosperité.

The knight.

When you see so costly a gold Chain
Worn by a man, who cannot be struck by criticism,
Know that this is a Knight of the order,
Having from the King such a singular gift.

The gentleman.

It is certain that the gallant Frenchman,
Of the Cavalry, is dressed in this way,
Whether you see him in this changeable style of dress,
His words and virtue are constant.

The Various Styles of Clothing

The damsel.

The women seen here are French Damsels,
With their affable and beautiful bearing,
Their conversation is agreeable to everyone,
And many of them have incomparable grace.

The Venetian.

Be certain that the Venetians,
(Who are Lords of noble and ancient lineage,)
While they are at the Palace, are dressed
As you see, and they are full of virtues.

The Various Styles of Clothing

The president of a tribunal.

Look at these clothes, which are without pomp or excess,
These are the clothes of solemn Presidents,
Who are appointed to judge proceedings,
By the King, at his Court residence.

The courtesan.

The French courtesan, as times go by,
Is gallant as you see by his appearance,
Many a woman he knows how to court,
Because with eloquence he shows propriety.

The Italian woman.

Look here at the woman from Italy,
As she is vividly shown in this present portrait
With her very pleasant and pretty appearance,
And with her love she attracts men.

The bourgeoise.

There is no woman who is prettier nor more courteous,
Showing herself to be chaste with her style of clothes,
It is in Paris, where there are many bourgeoises,
Such as the one vividly depicted here.

The Various Styles of Clothing

The bourgeois.

Here you can see the true Parisian,
His honest manner being in his way of dressing,
His mode of speaking is subtle, and average,
To trade goods, is in his very nature.

The old bourgeois.

If you want to see the old bourgeois of France,
His way of dressing, his gait and solemnity,
This portrait, depicting all of these things for you,
Is a little curious for its novelty.

The Various Styles of Clothing

The French artisan.

This is the artisan, dressed in his best cloak,
Loving his labor, with the aim of supporting himself,
He escapes idleness by hard work,
Because idleness is the source of all evils.

The scholar.

Here are the clothes that the scholar wears,
Making him look dignified as he is well known to be,
Calling himself protector of the faith.
Why is it that no one wants to believe him any longer?

The Various Styles of Clothing

The laborer.

The laborer is always very courageous,
In working for the landowner,
He is not proud; but concerning his work,
Often the well-fed are those, who do nothing.

The French soldier.

The true French soldier shows himself here,
Ready for battle, or for bravado,
But sometimes he abandons the inspection,
Or else [leaves] his host and country on the offensive.[1]

The Various Styles of Clothing

The footman.

Look at this footman [who is] light like the wind.
In order to run well, he does not have a dull appearance,
Most often he has no money in his purse,
Which is why he avoids paying his debts to his lord.

The French peasant woman.

Readers look carefully at the countenance,
Of the woman in this old-fashioned portrait,
It is common to see throughout France,
A peasant woman dressed in this way.

The Various Styles of Clothing

The woman of Picardy.

Take note of this woman with her old-fashioned bonnet,
This is the lively and honest woman of Picardy,
Her manner of speaking pleases, her appearance is not ugly,
But very often she is hot-tempered.

The French bride.

The bride has her hair arranged and is dressed,
As you see, when she takes a husband,
To show off her beauty which she has striven for,
On that day, not having a grieving heart.

The Various Styles of Clothing

The mourner.

Here are the clothes customary to the mourner,
Who wears black in color like darkness,
Sighing heavily, with tears in his eyes,
While the solemn funeral for the deceased takes place.

The man of Champagne.

If it is so that you recognize nothing,
About this present form and appearance,
Here are the true clothes of a man from Champagne,
Who appears vividly before your eyes.

The peasant of Bresse.

If you have never been to Bresse,
With this realistic and old-fashioned portrait,
You will be easily able to recognize from now on,
The authentic dress of a peasant woman from Bresse.

The woman of Brabant.

The woman of Brabant has a stiff manner here,
In this portrait which is simply composed,
Her outfit has a tucked up train,
And her hairstyle is like starched linen.

The Various Styles of Clothing

The Flemish girl.

Whoever asks to see a girl who is beautiful and youthful,
And dressed in her everyday clothes,
Must contemplate this Flemish girl,
In this very rigid style of dress.

The damsel of Flanders.

You should pay close attention to this portrait,
If you are not going to visit the country of Flanders,
Be assured that noble damsels,
In that place wear clothes like these.

The Various Styles of Clothing

The Dutch girl.

If you make an effort to look at this portrait,
In contemplating this girl's demeanor,
Without going to Holland, be certain,
That the Dutch girl is dressed in the way that is shown.

The woman of Holland.

The woman of Holland can most certainly,
Be clearly recognized in this figure,
Her dress is daintily pleated,
Clean and refined, she dresses according to her nature.

The Various Styles of Clothing

The English woman.

An English woman dresses like this,
The inside of her bonnet is lined with fur,
She is easily recognizable (even in foreign places)
By her square bonnet.

The Roman woman.

It is not necessary to go for a walk in Rome,
To see the gait, gesture, and solemnity,
Of a prudent old-fashioned Roman woman,
This portrait holds the truth of it.[2]

The Various Styles of Clothing

The woman of Lyons.

When you see before your eyes
The gallant woman of Lyon dressed like this,
It is better not to pick a quarrel in Lyons,
For it is cruel and fierce.

The woman with goiter.

Look at how the woman is like this,
With a huge neck suitable to a man,
Whether or not it is an admirable thing,
This portrait does not tell a single lie.

The man with goiter.

If you have been to the country of Piedmont
With this portrait you will be able to recognize,
That by going there and crossing the mountains
You could see a man like this with goiter.

The man of Provence.

Whoever has not been in warm Provence,
To see the manner and clothing [of the people],
Reflect upon the portrait before you,
In it you will see a genuine figure.

The Various Styles of Clothing

The Polish man.

If you are not familiar with this portrait,
With the wonderfully warm, fur-trimmed cap,
You will recognize that this is a Polish man,
Dreading the wind which beats at his ears.

The Scotsman.

It is necessary, reader, that you be entirely certain,
As soon as you see this portrait with your own eyes,
That these are the clothes that the Scotsman wears,
Which are neither too mundane nor too singular.[3]

The Scotswoman.

If you lower your eyes to this portrait
In order to better recognize the figure of a Scotswoman
The following conforms naturally,
As you see that it is portrayed true-to-life.

The savage of Scotland.

If you lower your eyes to this figure,
To this end you must be certain,
It is the savage from the country of Scotland,
Dressed in furs for protection against the cold.

The Various Styles of Clothing

Le capitaine sauuage.

Vous pourrez voir entre Les Escossoys
Tel capitaine faisant là leur scieurs
Qui souuent font nuysance aux Anglops
Peu & profit leur fait faire maints tours

The savage captain.

You will be able to see, living among
The Scottish, a captain such as this.
They often become a nuisance to the English
As little profit compels them to make many raids.

The Flemish man.

If you want to know about the clothes of a Flemish man,
His short robe and also his manner,
You will see by this portrait,
To change his style of clothes is not his worry.

The Various Styles of Clothing

The Flemish woman.

This portrait is made with the intention of
Showing a true-to-life Flemish woman.
If you do not go to these places: her clothing,
Is represented here in great detail.

The prior.

This monk is portrayed in good favor,
He is not cold because he is well-dressed,
And he has no desire to go hungry.
But he can not bear the cold weather.

The Various Styles of Clothing

The Carthusian monk.

Here are the authentically portrayed clothes,
Which are worn by the excessively wealthy Carthusian,
Who has the means to amass great temporal wealth,
Making him miserable.[4]

The canon.

Not only is a monk fat and vigorous,
[He is] well fed, comfortably bedded, well dressed.
But the rich canon is thus content,
Adorned with clothes and not with virtue.[5]

The monk.

The portrait that you see, depicts for you,
A true-to-life monk, holding his book in his hand.
If by chance he does not care for virtue,
To compensate he is dressed like this.

The old father of the village.

This old patron and father of the village
Is not inclined to change his style of clothes.
He would rather have a rich soup,
And his bed made up for him to sleep soundly.

The Various Styles of Clothing

The mourner of the village.

This is how the village woman dresses,
Bearing her mourning by wearing this garb
And in crying makes much more noise and racket
Than the priests commonly make.

The damsel in mourning.

In France the damsel dresses like this,
For her parents who are buried,
And she mourns with a natural zeal,
When she loses her friends.

The mourner of Flanders.

In Flanders women are taught,
To mourn according to a common practice,
In the same way that it is understood in life.
We see it with the present likeness of the portrait.

The man of Zeeland.

If you are prompted by a new interest,
To contemplate and know about the finery,
That the man of Zeeland is accustomed to,
You must contemplate it in this portrait.

The Various Styles of Clothing

The woman of Zeeland.

The woman of Zeeland in this portrait,
(In which you see her, shown in this way)
Can demonstrate to everyone apparently,
The way in which she dresses.

The bishop of the sea.

The land does not only have bishops,
Who are given great honor and title through [papal] bulls.
Likewise, the bishop springs up from the sea,
To say nothing about how many wear a miter.[6]

The Various Styles of Clothing

Le moyne de la mer.

La Mer poissons en abondance aporte
Par son diuin, que deuons estimer:
Mais fort estrange est le Moyne de Mer
Qui est ainsi que ce pourtrait le porte.

The monk of the sea.

The sea provides fish in abundance
By grace divine, which should be valued:
But extremely strange is the monk of the sea
Who is as this portrait conveys him to be.[7]

The standing ape.

Near Peru one can in effect see that
God gave the ape such a form,
Dressed in rattan, leaning on a walking stick,
Standing upright is something similar to man.

The Various Styles of Clothing

The Cyclops.

Ancient poets make mention of
Polyphemus and the Cyclopes.
It is said that this lineage continues yet,
With one eye as shown in this figure.[8]

The Swiss gentleman.

If you wish to be so curious,
Lower your eyes for a moment to this portrait.
Each person will certainly see how,
A gentleman is dressed in Switzerland.

The Various Styles of Clothing

The damsel of Switzerland.

To show you the clothes that damsels
Wear in Switzerland, it is in your interest to know,
That they all dress in this way,
As can be seen in this portrait.

The German foot soldier.

Day after day the German foot soldier adapts
To maintaining this old-fashioned style
Of his artless and suitable clothes,
And never avails himself of change.

The Various Styles of Clothing

The German woman foot soldier.

It is fitting to know that the foot soldier's wife also
Keeps up with the moving about. And such are her clothes,
As everyone can recognize here,
By looking at this portrait.

The woman of Germany.

The dress of the German woman is as such,
And does not change as often as ours does,
Because the French demand new clothes,
Changing them as often as the wind changes direction.

The Various Styles of Clothing

Le bourgeois allemant.

The bourgeois of Germany.

Notice the ingenuity of this style of dress,
These are the clothes of the German bourgeois,
Who like no others change their clothes.
Liking diversity is in their nature.

The man of Switzerland.

Here are the dress and the bearing of a man from Switzerland,
Influential and strong, for a long time as well,
The Kings of France have received service from them,
At court and in war, with contentment.

The Various Styles of Clothing

The woman of Switzerland.

Look closely at this way of dressing,
The whole shape and style as it is,
Because in Switzerland it is certain that
Every woman dresses like this always.

The woman of upper Germany.

If by chance someone asks you,
What this figure represents,
This is a real woman of upper Germany,
Portrayed true-to-life, according to nature.

The German girl.

Whenever you see hair as long as this,
Hanging down as you see here,
This is most certainly a German girl,
Dressed thus, you may be sure of it.

The Hungarian man.

If you are not overly curious,
About going out farther than your own lands,
Because of trouble along the way,
The man of Hungary is dressed in this manner.

The lady of Hungary.

Every lady living in Hungary,
Who has the honor of great lordship,
Always wears such a garb,
Which is very suitably depicted here.

The woman of Muscovy.

The woman of Muscovy as I have read,
Dresses in this manner, and with great elegance,
Having on her head a large fur hat,
Wearing skates which are rough shod for the ice.

The Various Styles of Clothing

The man of Muscovy.

The man of Muscovy with his long cloak
Wages war on the frozen sea,
And the desire which torments him even more
Is to acquire wealth on the land.

The woman of Bayonne.

The woman of Bayonne and her costume,
Can be contemplated here in this figure,
This style of dress does not change at all,
And she is simple by nature.

The woman going to mass.

The woman of Bayonne dresses in this manner.
Going to mass with great devotion,
She then returns home in all her finery,
Having received very little instruction.

The mourner of Bayonne.

Whenever it happens that a woman of Bayonne wears
Mourning clothes for her husband, or for a parent,
She is always dressed in this way,
As you see clearly in the portrait.

The Various Styles of Clothing

The peasant woman of Spain.

Spain is well cultivated and fertile:
As many things grow there successfully.
In this place the peasant woman dresses properly,
As is evident in this portrait.

The Basque man.

Look at the simple clothes of the Basque man.
He is more content in his suffering,
Than anyone dressed in lavish costumes,
As can be seen in the country of France.

The Various Styles of Clothing

The Basque woman.

This style of dress is not well-known,
The Basque woman is described here.
According to Basque custom her hair is shorn like this,
Demonstrating that she does not fear the cold.

The woman of Pamplona.

Here is the woman living in Pamplona,
Wearing her hat so. And she is always dressed
Without changing the style, as does the moon
In the way that the French do all the time.

The Various Styles of Clothing

The shorn woman of Spain.

Within Spain one sees a woman as such,
Who with hair shorn is taking part in such a pastime,
It is true that this is something profane:
Because several people take diversion in seeing her.[9]

The Spanish woman.

Whoever would like to know for certain,
How the woman of Spain is dressed,
It must certainly be thought that,
From a Spanish woman comes a fashionable image.

The Various Styles of Clothing

The Spanish man.

Whoever wishes to know about the dress and the bearing
Of the Spaniard must be completely certain,
That this portrait shows him in a true-to-life way,
Without going to see him in a country farther away.

The woman of Roncevalle.

If the hairstyle in this portrait,
Seems coarse to you,
Know that women of Roncevalle,
Wear their hair and are dressed in this manner.

The Various Styles of Clothing

The woman of Compostela.

The woman who comes from Compostela
Never goes anywhere without her hat.
And such is her style of dress, that
I do not know if you will find it becoming.

The woman of Toledo.

If your attention is fixed on this portrait,
It would be curious if you were not amazed by it.
The woman of Toledo is dressed like this,
Because it is the fashion of the country.

The Various Styles of Clothing

The Spanish peasant woman.

If you have frequented the villages
Of Spain, and heard the sound
Of the Nightingale, a woman at work
Has a similar way of dressing and moving.

The peasant woman of Portugal.

Among the fields of Portugal,
You will find a peasant woman like this.
Some lead their animals to graze in the fields,
And others do the work there.

The Various Styles of Clothing

The peasant woman of Hungary.

Every woman from the village
Of Hungarians, or wherever they stay,
Always wears this type of dress for everyday use,
From long ago until the present day.[10]

The Portuguese man.

The Portuguese man with his long cloak,
Does not fear a sudden accident at sea.
By trading he takes in great riches,
He is also very sober and diligent.

The Various Styles of Clothing

The Portuguese woman.

The Portuguese woman is dressed in this manner,
As she can be recognized in this portrait.
She has a great love of money,
As avarice, for her, has an attraction.

The man of Lübeck.

The man of Lübeck is natural to the hunt,
He dresses and wears boots in this mode.
It is not he who bids for silk,
Fashionable clothing is not a great concern.[11]

The Various Styles of Clothing

The woman of Lübeck.

The woman of Lübeck is not overly fond,
Of beautiful clothes, as one can see very well
In this portrait: but rather, curiously,
That she must have the necessities of life.

The woman of Barbary.

When the woman of Barbary in her most beautiful clothes,
Wants to prove her great magnificence,
She is wrapped in copious furs,
Which is apparent in this portrait.

The Various Styles of Clothing

The man of Barbary.

Men of Barbary have clothes similar to these,
As you see that this is well-known.
Whether these clothes seem admirable to you,
The truth obliges you to believe it.

The Moorish woman.

The Moorish woman resembles the black Moor.
Her dress is lightweight for the heat.
The man and woman go well together,
The two having flat noses and black skin.

The Various Styles of Clothing

The Moorish man.

The Moorish man dresses lightly in this manner,
Because of the heat which is endured in this country.
He likewise has a flat nose,
His hair is curly, his lips are full and unyielding.

The savage woman.

The savage woman to the human eye is unimaginable,
She is like this in her natural surroundings,
Depicted for you in a life-like way,
As it appears before your eyes.

The Various Styles of Clothing

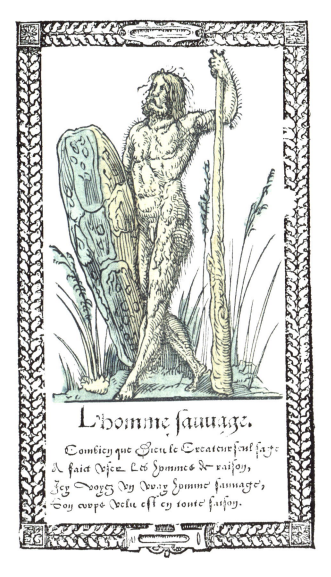

The savage man.

How much has God the Creator, who alone is wise,
Made use of men of reason.
Here, look at a true savage man.
His body is covered with hair in every season.

The man of India.

Concerning the Indian and his strange dress,
From this portrait you can see the truth.
If you do not believe it, I say for [confirmation],
Go as far as this place and you will be able to see him.[12]

The woman of India.

Dear reader, it is fitting for you to hear,
That the Indian woman is suitably dressed.
This clothing can be understood here,
Because it is simply portrayed.

The Persian man.

From Persia come ancient peoples.
From them one sees much recorded history.
The costume of the Persian is such
As you see it in this portrait.

The Various Styles of Clothing

The Persian woman.

If you would like to catch sight of a Persian woman,
Her bearing and her everyday dress,
You would not be able to see her more clearly
Than she is portrayed and restricted here.

The Egyptian man.

To easily recognize a true Egyptian,
With his long dishevelled hair,
Clinging to his old-fashioned clothing.
He is portrayed true-to-life in this way.

The Various Styles of Clothing

The Egyptian woman.

It is certain that the Egyptian woman,
Up until today wears her clothes in this way.
Such was her costume of long ago,
As you see it now with your own eyes.

The hermit of Egypt.

Thus dresses the Egyptian hermit,
Who makes himself a stranger to the common people here.
Eating roots, acting as a sycophant,
If he found better, he would like to eat it.

The Various Styles of Clothing

The priest of Egypt.

This long hat, the long beard also,
Represents for us the Egyptian priest,
Who has less concern about the true God
Than for the gifts which are presented to him at the temple.

The savage on display.

When the savage is boasting or displaying,
He is suitably dressed like this.
If you are afraid that this portrait deceives you,
Go to these places to see his clothes.

The Various Styles of Clothing

Le tartare.

The Tartar.

If this portrait seems uncouth to some,
For those who have not seen him as he is depicted,
It is certain that the Tartar is as such,
And that these clothes are real, and not imagined.

The Brazilian woman.

The women there dress like this,
Which this portrait shows and represents.
There, monkeys, and parrots also,
Are put up for sale to strangers by the women.

The Various Styles of Clothing

The Brazilian man.

The man from the place where the Brazil tree grows,
Is such as he appears before your eyes.
He applies himself to the natural work of
Cutting down Brazil trees in order to trade them.

The woman of Nicteroy.

If you cast your eyes at times
On this portrait, which can seem strange,
Believe that these are old-fashioned clothes,
Which the wife of this Nictorian wears.[13]

The Various Styles of Clothing

The man of Nicteroy.

Whoever would like to see how a man from Nicteroy
Wears his hair and dresses, here he appears.
And from change he guards himself well,
For as long as he lives in this world.

The Turkish girl.

The Turks live far away, so it is not necessary to go there
To better understand the kind of clothes they wear.
But to recognize a Turkish girl,
The clothes that she wears are portrayed here.

The Various Styles of Clothing

The girl of Africa.

From this portrait which is rather ancient,
You can see a girl of Africa,
Who wears for finery a small cloak,
Lined with an exquisite pelt.

The Greek man.

The Greek man has clothes which are similar to these.
This image of him is well-known,
Whether it seems to you that these clothes are admirable,
The truth compels you to believe it.

The Various Styles of Clothing

The Greek woman.

The Greek woman also has her costume,
And her bearing is equally elegant.
And her hair-style is kept up prettily:
But her countenance is too polite and forced.

The Janissary man.

You see the genuine portrait of Janissaries,
Who come from the great country of Turkey,
Where the means that are necessary
In order to serve it are readily known.

The Various Styles of Clothing

The Janissary woman.

The Janissary woman wears her clothing just as
This portrait shows and figures it.
She wears a pointed hat, and also,
Dresses in a long veil.

The Greek serving the Turks.

Here is the portrait of the proud Greek.
I understand that those who are in military service of Turkey,
Are inclined by their nature
To do battle as much by sea as by land.[14]

The Various Styles of Clothing

The Turkish footman.

This Turkish footman is here, without lying,
Depicted in a life-like way as everyone can see,
This is the way in which he dresses,
In order to run better, which he is ready to do.

The Lady of Turkey.

The ladies of Turkey are thus,
Dressed as you see them here.
Their demeanor, their dress, their countenance,
Are all shown in the present image.

The Various Styles of Clothing

The Turkish man.

Without doubting it, and without deceiving you,
You must believe that the dress of a Turkish man,
In the present image and portrait,
Resembles that which one can see in real life.

The Arabian man.

In Arabia there is an abundance of frankincense.
Arabians of long ago were rich,
And this portrait shows you evidence of
The proper dress that they wear, and wore in the past.

The Arabian woman.

If you want to have an understanding of a woman,
Who is a native of Arabia,
This figure shows you evidence of
The style of dress worn by the women.

The woman of Asia.

Look carefully at how Asian women
Are dressed, and have their hair neatly styled.
I am certain that the Venetians
Could not have found any fault in this.

The Various Styles of Clothing

The clothed woman of Africa.

Whenever an African woman has lost her husband,
Being in death held tightly in the coffin,
Such are the clothes she wears in mourning,
Showing that she has a grieving heart.[15]

NOTES

1. The word *le paye* in the fourth line has been translated as country, even though it is not found with the e-ending in historical or modern dictionaries.

2. The word *pourmaint* does not appear in either historical or modern French dictionaries. I have translated the word as *se promener* since it appears as *se pourmener* in Huguet's *Dictionnaire de la langue Française du Seiziène Siècle* (p. 116, vol. 6, Didier, Paris 1965).

3. In the translation of the fourth line I have changed the word *par* to *pas*.

4. The Carthusian order was established by Bruno of Cologne in 1084. The aescetic practices of the monks included living in total silence, following a strict diet, and wearing a hair shirt. The order was supported through agriculture, raising sheep for wool and through donations from wealthy benefactors. Since the monks were forbidden contact with the secular world, lay brothers or *convers* managed the business affairs of the charter house, as well as doing the manual labor. The last two lines of the poem make reference to the wretchedness of living an aescetic life, despite the great wealth accumulated by the order (*Dictionary of the Middle Ages*. ed. Joseph R. Strayer, vol. 3. New York: Charles Scribner's Sons, 1983. pp. 118-119).

5. I have translated the word *refait* in the first line as vigorous, instead of using the literal translation of renewed.

6. The bishop of the sea bears a striking resemblance to the woodcut illustration made by the Swiss naturalist Konrad Gesner (1516-1565). According to Gesner, the bishop-like sea monster had been sighted off of the coast of Poland in 1531 (*Curious Woodcuts of Fanciful and Real Beasts: a Selection of 190 Sixteenth-Century Woodcuts from Gesner's and Topsell's Natural Histories*. New York: Dover Publications, Inc., 1971, p. 2). The original woodcut can be found in *Nomenclator Aquatilium Animantium. Icones animalium in mari & dulcilus aquis degentium . . . per Conradum Gesnerum Tigurinum . . .* published by Christoph. Froschoverus in Zurich, 1560. [First Edition].

7. This monk-like monster also appeared previously in Konrad Gesner's *Nomenclatur Aquatilium* [1560]. This type of creature was reported to have been caught off of the coast of Norway in Gesner's life time.

8. In Greek mythology the Cyclopes were one-eyed giants, who made thunderbolts for Zeus. One of them was Polyphemus, son of Poseidon (*Fabulous Beasts and Demons* by Heiny Mode. England: Phantom, 1975. p. 209).

9. Some of those who were found guilty during the Spanish Inquisition were accused of being sorcerers. In *L'Administration de la Foi: L'Administration de Tolède XVIè-XVIIIè siecle*, (Madrid: Casa de Velázquez, 1989), Jean-Pierre Dedicu writes that sorcerers were thought to have met in groups in a field or house at night and taking part in profane acts, such as dancing to the sound of a tambourine. p. 323.

10. In the fourth line the word "la" is most likely a shortened version of *il ya*.

11. The place name Delubic does not appear in modern or historical atlases. It is possible that Deserps was referring to the trading town of Lübeck on the north-

ern coast of Germany. I have translated "ia" in the fourth line as the pronoun "il".

12. The word *marevange* does not appear in standard French dictionaries. I translated the word to mean confirmation or proof of something.

13. Nicteroy is now Rio de Janerio.

14. I have translated the word *Gregois* in the first line as Greek since the person or place name in the title of the other poems has been repeated in the first or second line of the poems. It is possible that *Gregois* was meant to be *gregeois* as in *feu grégeois* or Greek fire. *The Oxford English Dictionary* defines Greek fire as "a combustible composition for setting fire to an enemy's ships . . . so called by first being used by the Greeks in Constantinople" (*The Oxford English Dictionary*, vol. IV, Oxford: Clarendon Press, 1933, p. 239).

15. I have translated the word *vesue* in the title as *vestue* or dressed.

TRANSCRIPTIONS

Le chevalier.

Qand vous verrez un si riche Collier
Porter à l'homme, ou blame ne peult mordre
Pensez que c'est un Chevalier de l'ordre,
Ayant du Roy un don tant singulier.
p 35.

Le gentilhomme.

Il est certain que le brave françois,
A la Reistre, il s'est du tout vestu,
Si en habit mobile tu le vois,
Il est constant en parolle et vertu.
p 36.

La damoyselle.

Celles on voit françoises Damoyselles,
En leur maintien gracieuses et belles,
Leur entretien à tous est agreable,
Et pleines sont de grace incomparable.
p 37.

Le venitien.

Soyez certains que les Venitiens,
(Qui sont Seigneurs nobles et anciens,)
Alors qu'ils vont au Palais, sont vestus,
Comme voyez et sont pleins de vertus.
p 38.

Le president.

Voit cest habit, sans pompe ny exces,
C'est la vesture des graves Presidens,
Qui sont commis à juger les proces,
De par le Roy, en sa Court residens.
p 39.

Le courtisan.

Le Courtisan françois, au temps qui court,
Est brave ainsi qu'en voyez la figure,
A mainte dame il sçait faire la Court,
Car d'eloquence il entend la mesure.
p 40.

L'italienne.

Voyez icy la femme d'Italie,
Comme elle est vive en ce present pourtrait
De sa façon fort plaisante et jolie,
A son amour les hommes elle attrait.
p 41.

La bourgeoise.

Femme on ne voit plus belle ni plus courtoise,
Ce monstrant chaste avec son vestement,
Que dans Paris, ou est mainte bourgeoise,
Telle qu'elle est paincte icy vivement.
p 42.

Le bourgeois.

Tu peux voir cy le vray Parisien,
Sa mode honneste estant en sa vesture,
Son parler est subtil, et a moyen,
De trafiquer, c'est sa propre nature.
p 43.

Le vieil bourgeois.

Si tu veux voir le vieil bourgeois de France,
Le sien habit son port et gravité,
Ce pourtraict cy, t'en fait la demonstrance
Peu curieux est de nouvelleté.
p 44.

L'artisan francois.

C'est l'artisan, vestu de bonne cape,
Aymant labeur, à fin qu'il s'en nourrisse,
Oysiveté par travail il eschappe,
Pource que c'est de tous maux la Nourrice.
p 45.

Le docteur.

Voicy l'habit que porte le docteur,
Faisant le grave ainsi qu'il est notoire,
Luy ce disant de la foy protecteur,
D'ou vient cela? qu'on ne le veult plus croire.
p 46.

Le laboureur.

Le laboureur a tousjours bon courage,
De travailler au Monde terrien,
Il n'est oysist; mais de son labourage,
Souvent nourris sont ceux, qui ne font rien.
p 47.

Le souldat francois.

Le vray souldat François icy se monstre,
Prest pour combatre, ou pour faire bravades,
Mais quelque fois il remet à la Monstre,
Son hoste, ou bien le paye en bastonnades.
p 48.

Le lacquais.

Voit ce lacquais leger comme le vent.
Pour bien courir, il n'a la couleur fade,
Argent il n'a en bource le plus souvent,
Par quoy son hoste est payé en gambade.
p 49.

La rusticque francoise.

Regardez bien lecteurs la contenance,
De ceste femme en ce pourtrait anticque,
Tousjours ainsi on voit parmy la France,
Estre vestue une femme rusticque.
p 50.

La picarde.

Voy ceste femme avec son Bavolet,
C'est la picarde esveillee et honeste,
Son parler plaist, son maintien n'est pas laid
Mais bien souvent elle a mauvaise teste.
p 51.

Lepousee de france.

Lepousee est coiffee aussi vestue,
Comme voyez, quant elle prent mary,
A demonstrer sa beauté s'evertue,
En ce jour là, n'ayant le cueur marry.
p 52.

Le dueil.

Voicy l'habit accoustumé au dueil,
Noir de couleur comme sont les tenebres,
Quand par souspirs avecques larmes, d'œil,
Pour les defuncts on faict pompes funebres.
p 53.

Le champenoys.

S'il est ainsi que rien tu ne cognoys,
En ceste forme et figure presente,
Voicy le vray habit d'un Champenoys,
Qui a tes yeux vivement se presente.
p 54.

La rusticque de brece.

S'y n'a esté en la Brece jamais,
Par ce pourtrait naturel et anticque,
Tu pourras bien cognoistre desormais,
Le vray habit d'une Brece rusticque.
p 55.

La brebansonne.

La Brebansonne est icy compassee,
Par ce pourtraict au naif composé,
Son vestement à la queue troussee,
Et la coiffure est de linge empesé.
p 56.

La fille flamende.

Qui fille belle et freche voir demande,
Et habillee en habit usité,
Doit contempler ceste fille Flamende,
En cest habit vivement limité.
p 57.

La damoiselle flamende.

Pour ce pourtrait vous faire mieux entendre,
Si vous n'allez voir le pays de Flandre,
Assurez vous que nobles Damoyselles,
En ce lieu là portent vestures telles.
p 58.

La fille holandoise.

Sur ce pourtrait si ton œil s'evertue,
En contemplant ceste fille au maintien,
Sans en Holande aller, pour certain tien,
Que tout ainsi: la fille y est vestue.
p 59.

La holandoise.

La Holandoise on peult certainement,
Bien recognoistre en icelle figure,
Son habit est plissé mignonnement,
Blanche et polie elle est de sa nature.
p 60.

L'angloise.

Ainsi vestue est une femme Angloise,
Par le dedans son bonnet est fourré,
On la cognoist (bien qu'au lieux on ne voise)
Facilement à son bonnet carré.
p 61.

La romaine.

Il ne faut pas qu'à Rome on se pourmaint,
Pour voir le port, le geste, et gravité,
D'une prudente et antique Romaine,
Ce pourtrait cy, en tien la verité.
p 62.

La lyonnoise.

Quand vous verrez la brave Lyonnoise,
Vestue ainsi au plus pres de voz yeux,
Mieux vaut que prendre à Lyon noise,
Pour ce qu'il est cruel et furieux.
p 63.

La gouestre.

Voyez comment ceste femme est semblable,
En grosse gorge à l'homme proprement,
Quoy que ce soit une chose admirable,
Ce pourtrait cy ne ment aucunement.
p 64.

Le gouestre.

Si as esté au pays de Piedmont
Par ce pourtrait tu pourras recognoistre
Qu'en y allant et traversant les Mont
Tu as peu voir de semblable gouestre.
p 65.

Le provencal.

Qui n'a esté en la chaude Provence,
Pour voir l'habit et la vesture,
La contempler ce pourtrait cy t'avance,
Au naturel en verras la figure.
p 66.

Le pollognoys.

Si ce pourtrait icy tu ne cognoys,
Au chapperon fourré, chaud à merveilles,
Tu cognoistras que c'est un Pollognoys,
Craignant le vent qui le frappe aux aureilles.
p 67.

L'escossois.

Il faut lecteur que tout certain tu sois,
Quant tu verras ce pourtrait de tes yeux,
Que c'est l'habit que porte l'escossois,
Qui n'est par trop mondain ne curieux.*
p 68.

L'escossoise.

Si vous baissez l'œil dessus ce pourtrait
Pour bien sçavoir d'Escossoise la forme
Cestuy cy est au naturel conforme,
Comme voyez qu'au vif il est pourtrait.
p 69.

La sauvage d'escosse.

Si tu mets l'œil dessus ceste figure,
A celle fin que certain tu en soys,
C'est la sauvage au pays Escossoys,
De peaux vestue encontre la froidure.
p 70.

Le capitaine sauvage.

Vous pourrez voir entre les Escossoys,
Tel capitaine faisant là leur sejours,
Qui font souvent nuysance aux Angloys
Peu de profit leur fait faire maints tours.
p 71.

Le flament.

Si du Flament veut sçavoir la vesture
Sa courte robe et sa maniere aussi,
Tu le verras par ceste pourtraiture,
Changer d'habit ce n'est point son soucy.
p 72.

La flamende.

Au vif tiree est ceste pourtraiture,
D'une Flamende ainsi expressement,
Si sur les lieux vous n'allez: sa vesture,
Est peincte icy labourieusement.
p 73.

Le prieur.

Pourtrait est ce moine en bon point,
Il n'a pas froid par faute de vesture,
Et endurer la faim il ne veut point,
Or il ne peut endurer la froidure.
p 74.

Le chartreux.

Voicy l'habit pourtrait au naturel,
Dont est vestu le trop riche Chartreux,
Qui d'amasser, un grand bien temporel,
Sçait le moyen, faisant le marmiteux.
p 75.

Le chanoine.

Gras et refait n'est seulement un moine
Fort bien nourry, bien couché, bien vestu:
Mais ainsi aise est le riche chanoine,
Garny d'habits et non pas de vertu.
p 76.

Le moyne.

Ce pourtrait cy que voyez, vous delivre,
Du moyne au vif, ayant en main son livre.
Si d'aventure il n'ayme la vertu,
Pour recompense il est ainsi vestu.
p 77.

Le vieil pere de village.

Ce vieil patron et pere de village
N'est pas enclin de ses habits changer,
Mieux aymeroit avoir de gras potage,
Et son lict fait pour molement coucher.
p 78.

Le dueil de village.

Voyla comment se vest la villageoise,
Portant le dueil en cest accoustrement
Et en plorant fait plus grand bruit et noise
Que ne font pas prestres communement.
p 79.

La damoiselle en dueil.

En France ainsi se vest la damoiselle,
Pour ses parens en sepulture mis,
Et fait son dueil par un naturel zele,
Quand elle a fait perte de ses amis.
p 80.

Le dueil de flandre.

En Flandre ont les femmes apris,
Faire dueil en commun usage,
Ainsi qu'au vif nous le voyons compris
Par le pourtrait de la presente image.
p 81.

Le zelandoys.

Si tu es meu d'une nouvelle cure,
De contempler et sçavoir la parure,
Accoustimee à l'homme Zelandoys,
En ce pourtrait contempler tu la doys.
p 82.

La zelandoyse.

La Zelandoyse en ce pourtrait icy,
(Ou tu la voys, estre exprimee ainsi)
Peut à chacun monstrer apertement,
Quelle façon est en son vestement.
p 83.

L'evesque de mer.

La terre n'a evesques seulement,
Qui sont par bule en grand honneur et tiltre
L'evesque croist en mer semblablement,
Ne parlant point, combien qu'il port mitre.
p 84.

Le moyne de la mer.

La Mer poissons en abondance aporte
Par don divin, que devons estimer:
Mais fort estrange est le Moyne de Mer
Qui est ainsi que ce pourtrait le porte.
p 85.

Le singe debout.

Pres le Peru par effect le voit on,
Dieu à donné au Singe telle forme,
Vestu de jonc, s'apuyant d'un baton,
Estant debout chose aux hommes conforme.
p 86.

Le ciclope.

De Polipheme et des Siclopiens,
Font mention poetes anciens,
Ont dit encor que ce lignage dure,
Avec un œil selon ceste figure.
p 87.

Le gentilhomme suysse.

Si vous voulez estre tant curieux,
D'un peu baisser sur ce pourtrait voz yeux
Certainement un chacun verra comme,
En Suysse est vestu un gentilhomme.
p 88.

La damoiselle suysse.

Pour vous monstrer l'habit que Damoiselles,
Ont en Suysse, il vous convient sçavoir,
Qu'en vestement elles sont toutes telles,
Qu'en ce pourtrait on peut apercevoir.
p 89.

Le lansquenet.

Le Lansquenet jour en jour s'acommode,
A l'entretien de ceste vieille mode,
De son naif et propre habillement,
Et sans jamais user de changement.
p 90.

La lansquenette.

Croire convient la Lansquenette aussi,
Tenir ce geste, et telle est sa vesture,
Comme chacun le peut cognoistre icy,
Par le regard de ceste pourtraiture.
p 91.

L'alemande.

L'habit est tel de la femme Alemande,
Et point ne change ainsi que nous souvent,
Car le François nouveaux habits demande,
En les muant ainsi comme le vent.
p 92.

Le bourgeois allemant.

De c'est habit voyez l'invention,
C'est du bourgeois Allemant la vesture,
Qui comme aucuns n'en fait mutation,
Diversité aymans de leur nature.
p 93.

Le suysse.

Voicy l'habit et geste de Suysse,
Puissant et fort, ainsi que des long temps,
Les Roys de France en ont tiré service,
En Court et guerre, avec desire contens.
p 94.

La suysse.

Regardez bien de c'est habillement,
Toute la forme et façon comme elle est
Car en Suysse ainsi certainement,
Chacune femme ainsi tousjours se vest.
p 95.

La haulte allemande.

Si d'aventure on vous demande,
Que represente ceste figure,
C'est une vraye haulte Allemande,
Pourtraite au vif selon nature.
p 96.

La fille allemande.

Quant vous verrez chevelure ainsi grand
Pendre du chef, comme icy la voyez,
C'est pour certain une fille Allemand,
Vestue ainsi de ce seur en soyez.
p 97.

Le hongre.

Si ne voulez estre trop curieux,
De cheminer jusques aux propres lieux,
Pour du chemin fuir la fascherie,
Ainsi se vest l'homme de Hongrie.
p 98.

La dame de hongrie.

Chacune Dame habitant en Hongrie,
Qui a l'honneur de grande Seigneurie,
Porte tousjours un tel accoustrement,
Qu'il est icy depaint fort proprement.
p 99.

La mosquonide.

La mosquonide ainsi comme j'ai leu,
Se vest ainsi et d'une bonne grace,
Ayant en teste un gros chapeau velu,
Portant patins qui sont ferrez à glace.
p 100.

Le mosquonide.

Le mosquonide avec sa grande mante
Dessus la mer gelee fait la guerre,
Et le desir qui plus fort le tourmente
C'est d'acquerir des biens dessus la terre.
p 101.

La femme de bayonne.

La Bayonnoise et son accoustrement,
On peut icy contempler en figure,
De cest habit ne change aucunement,
Et simple elle est de sa propre nature.
p 102.

La femme allant a la messe.

La femme ainsi en Bayonne à vesture,
Oyant la messe en grand devotion,
Puis s'en revient avec ceste parure,
Ayant receu bien peu d'instruction.
p 103.

Le dueil de bayonne.

Quant il avient que Bayonnoise porte
L'habit de dueil pour mary, ou parent,
Elle est tousjours vestue en ceste sorte
Comme voyez au pourtrait apparent.
p 104.

La rusticque d'espaigne.

Hespaigne est fort plantureuse et fertile:
Car mainte chose y croist heureusement,
Femme Rusticque en ce lieu proprement,
Comme il appert en ce pourtrait s'habille.
p 105.

Le bisquin.

Voy du Bisquin le simple habillement,
Plus content est avec sa souffrance,
Qu'aucun vestu de riche accoustrement,
Que l'on peut voir par le pays de France.
p 106.

La bisquine.

Ceste vesture est bien peu entendue,
La Bisquine est depainte en cest endroit,
Par sa coustume elle est ainsi tondue,
En demonstrant qu'elle ne crains pas le froid.
p 107.

La femme de pampelune.

Voicy la femme estant en Pampelune,
Coiffee ainsi, et vestue tousjours,
Sans point changer l'habit, comme la Lune,
Ainsi que font les François tous les jours.
p 108.

La tondue d'espaigne.

Dedans l'Espaigne on voit de telle femme,
Qui tondue sont faisant tel passetemps,
Vray est que c'est une chose profane:
Car plusieurs gens à le voir passetemps.
p 109.

L'espaignolle.

Qui bien voudra cognoistre seurement,
Comme en Espaigne est la femme habillee
Il doit penser qu'icy certainement,
D'une Espaignolle est l'image taillee.
p 110.

L'espaignol.

Qui veut sçavoir et l'habit et le geste,
De l'Espaignol faut estre tout certain,
Que ce pourtrait au vif le manifeste,
Sans l'aller voir en pays plus loingtain.
p 111.

La femme de roncevalle.

Si la coiffure vous semble salle,
Que voyez en ce pourtrait cy,
Sachez que femme à Roncevalle,
Sont coiffee et vestue ainsi.
p 112.

La femme de compostelle.

Femme qui est du lieu de Compostelle
Ne va jamais sans porter son chapeau,
Et son habit est d'une façon telle,
Je ne sçay pas s'il vous semblera beau.
p 113.

La femme de tollete.

Si ton regard sur ce pourtrait s'arreste,
Estrange il estimais ne t'en esbahis,
La femme ainsi est vestue en Tollete,
Pource que c'est la façon du pays.
p 114.

L'espaignolle rusticque.

Si vous avez frequenté le village,
Parmy l'Espaigne, en escoutant le son,
Du Rossignol, femme de labourage,
D'habit et geste a semblable façon.
p 115.

La rusticque de portugal.

En Portugal parmy les lieux champestres,
Y trouverez de semblable rusticque,
Les une au champs mene leur beste paistre,
Et au labeur les autres s'y applicque.
p 116.

La rusticque de hongrie.

Chacune femme estant par le village
Des Hongriens ou elles font sejour,
Porte tousjours cest habit pour usage,
Ia des long temps jusque au present jour.*
p 117.

Le portugais.

Le Portugais avecques sa grand chape,
Ne crains de mer le soudain accident,
Par traffiquer grand richesse il attrape,
Aussi est il fort sobre et diligent.
p 118.

La portugaise.

La Portugaise est vestue en la sorte,
Que la pouvez cognoistre à ce pourtrait,
Fort grand amour à l'argent elle porte:
Car avarice à ce desir l'attrait.
p 119.

Le delubic.

Le Delubic naturel à la proye,
Se vest, et chausse en ceste mode cy,
Ce n'est point luy qui enchery la soye,
D'habit mondain ia n'est en grand soucy.
p 120.

La delubicque.

La Delubicque n'est pas trop amoureuse,
De beaux habits comme bien on peut voir,
Par ce pourtrait: mais plustost curieuse,
De vivre avoir dont elle fait devoir.
p 121.

La barbare.

Quand la Barbare en ses habits plus beaux,
Veut demonstrer sa grand magnificence,
Fourree ainsi elle est de riches peaux,
Que ce pourtrait le met en apparence.
p 122.

Le barbare.

Les Barbares ont le vestement semblable,
Comme tu vois cela est tout notoire,
Quoy que te soit c'est habit admirable,
La verité te contraint de le croire.
p 123.

La moresque.

Au More noir la Moresque ressemble,
Son habit est leger pour la chaleur,
L'homme et la femme accordent bien ensemble,
Tous deux camus et de noire couleur.
p 124.

Le more.

Le More se vest ainsi legerement,
Pour la chaleur du pays qu'il endure,
Le nez camus, il a semblablement,
Son poil frison, sa levre espaisse et dure.
p 125.

La femme sauvage.

Femme sauvage à l'œil humain non fainte,
Ainsi qu'elle est sur le naturel lieu,
Au naturel vous est icy depainte,
Comme voyez qu'il apert a vostre œil.
p 126.

L'homme sauvage.

Combien que Dieu le Createur seul sage
A faict user les hommes de raison,
Icy voyez un vray homme sauvage,
Son corps velu est en toute saison.
p 127.

L'indien.

De l'Indien et son habit estrange,
Par ce pourtrait la verité peut voir.
Si ne le croys, je dis pour marevange,
Va jusqu'au lieu et tu le pourras voir.
p 128.

L'indienne.

Amy lecteur, il te convient entendre,
Que l'Indienne est vestue proprement,
De cest habit que peux icy comprendre,
Pource qu'il est pourtrait naifuement.
p 129.

Le persien.

De Perse sont les peuples anciens,
D'eux mainte histoire on voit par escriture,
Le propre habit est tel des Persiens,
Que le voyez en ceste pourtraiture.
p 130.

La persienne.

Si vous voulez le geste appercevoir,
De Persienne, et sa robe usitee,
Vous ne pourriez plus clairement la voir,
Qu'elle est icy pourtraite et limitee.
p 131.

L'egyptien.

Pour bien cognoistre un vray Egyptien
Avec les longs cheveux espars qu'il porte,
En retenant son habit ancien,
Il est au vif pourtrait en ceste sorte.
p 132.

L'egyptienne.

Il est certain qu'ainsi l'Egyptienne,
Jusqu'au jourd'huy porte son vestement,
Telle a esté sa coustume ancienne,
Comme vostre œil le voit presentement.
p 133.

L'hermite d'egyte.

Ainsi se vest l'Egyptien hermite,
Qui du commun icy se rend estranger,
Mangeant racine faisant la chatemite,
S'il trouvoit mieux, il en voudroit manger.
p 134.

Le prestre d'egypte.

Ce long chapeau, la longue barbe aussi,
L'Egyptien prestre nous represente,
Qui du vray Dieu n'a pas tant de soucy,
Que de ces dons qu'au temple on luy presente.
p 135.

Le sauvage en pompe.

Quand le Sauvage est en bravade ou pompe,
Il est ainsi habillé proprement,
Si tu as peur que ce pourtrait te trompe,
Va sur les lieux pour voir son vestement.
p 136.

Le tartare.

Si ce pourtrait à ceux semble barbare,
Qui ne l'ont veu qu'ainsi qu'il est depainct,
Il est tout seur que tel est le Tartare,
Et cest habit est vray, et non pas fainct.
p 137.

La bresilienne.

Les femmes là sont vestues ainsi,
Que ce pourtrait le monstre et represente,
Là des Guenons, et perroquets aussi,
Aux estrangers elles mettent en vente.
p 138.

Le bresilien.

L'homme du lieu auquel le bresil croist,
Est tel qu'icy à l'œil il apparoist,
Leur naturel exercice s'aplique,
Coupper bresil pour en faire trafique.
p 139.

La nictorienne.

Si quelquefois vostre regard se range,
Sur ce pourtrait qui peut sembler estrange,
Croyez que c'est un habit ancien,
Que porte femme à ce Nictorien.
p 140.

Le nictorien.

Qui voudra voir comme un Nictorien,
Se coiffe et vest en voicy la figure,
Et de changer il se garde fort bien,
Tant que vivant en ce monde il dure.
p 141.

La fille turquoise.

Les Turcs sont loin, point ne faut qu'on y voise,
Pour mieux sçavoir de leur habit la sorte,
Mais pour cognoistre une fille Turquoise,
Icy pourtrait est l'habit qu'elle porte.
p 142.

La fille d'affrique.

Par ce pourtrait qui est assez antique,
Vous povez voir une fille d'Affrique,
Qui pour parure a son petit manteau,
Estant fourré d'une exquise peau.
p 143.

Le grec.

Le Grec il a un vestement semblable,
A ce pourtrait cela est tout notoire,
Quoy que te semble c'est habit admirable,
La verité te contriant de le croire.
p 144.

La grecque.

La Grecque aussi a son accoustrement
Et son maintient d'une assez bonne grace
Et sa coiffure entretient joliment:
Mais taxee est de trop polir sa face.
p 145.

Le janissaire.

Tu voys le vray pourtrait des Janissaires,
Qui du grand Turc ont leur nourrissement,
Pour le servir des choses necessaires,
Ou il cognoist prompt leur entendement.
p 146.

La janissaire.

La Janissaire a sa vesture ainsi,
Que ce pourtrait le monstre et le figure,
Chapeau pointu elle porte, et aussi,
Vestue elle est d'une longue vesture.
p 147.

Le grec servant le turc.

Du fier Gregois voicy la pourtraiture,
J'entend de ceux qui en l'art militaire,
Servent le Turc enclinant leur nature,
A guerroyer tant par mer que par terre.
p 148.

Le laquais turc.

Ce laquais Turc est icy sans mentir,
Au vif depaint comme un chacun peut voir,
C'est le moyen qu'il a de soy vestir,
Pour mieux courir, dont il fait prompt devoir.
p 149.

La dame de turquie.

Les dames sont en la Turquie ainsi,
Comme voyez vestue ceste cy,
Tout leur maintien, leur habit, leur visage,
Est exprimé par la presente image.
p 150.

Le turc.

Sans en doubter, et sans vous decevoir,
Devez penser que d'un Turc la vesture,
Ressemble au vif à celle qu'on peut voir,
En la presente image et pourtraiture.
p 151.

L'arabien.

En Arabie est d'encens abondance,
Arabiens jadis riches estoyent,
Et ce pourtrait vous met en evidence,
Le propre habit qu'ils portent, et qu'ils portoyent.
p 152.

L'arabienne.

Sy veux de femme avoir la cognoissance,
Qui d'Arabie à pris nativité,
Ceste figure te mets en evidence,
L'habit qui est par les femmes porté.
p 153.

La femme d'asie.

Regardez bien comment les Asiennes,
Sont habillees et coiffees en bonne ordre,
Je suis certain que les Veniciennes,
N'y pourroyent pas sur ce trouver à mordre.
p 154.

La vesue d'affrique.

Quant l'Affriquaine a perdu son mary
Estant par mort serré dans le sercueil,
Tel vestement elle porte par dueil,
En demonstrant qu'elle a le cœur marry.
p 155.